The Singing Garden

The Singing Garden

A STUDY OF THE BOOK OF PSALMS

DARREN CUSHMAN WOOD

North United Methodist Church ● Indianapolis, IN

ISBN 979-8-9882332-3-7 (epub)

ISBN 979-8-9882332-4-4 (paperback)

The cover art comes from a small portion of one of the many beautiful banners throughout North United Methodist Church created by the late Doris Douglas, a long-time member, and other artists.

Contents

Introduction

In the fourth century the Egyptian Bishop Athanasius sent a letter to a fellow Christian named Marcellinus recommending that he start his study of scripture by reading the Psalms. The psalms are the best place to start, according to the bishop, because they are prayers, they contain the wide array of biblical themes, and they are set to music. Athanasius likened the book to a garden: "The Book of Psalms is like a garden containing things of all these kinds, and it sets them to music."

The psalms are a "singing garden" that has been fruitful for generations of believers. Jesus quoted the psalms often, and the letter to the Hebrews is a collection of sermons based on the psalms. For centuries they were the only songs sung in the church. (In fact, the emergence of modern hymns was rejected, at first, by some traditions because they were not psalms.) When they recovered his briefcase from the plane crash in 1961 in Zambia, Dag Hammarskjöld, the secretary-general of the United Nations, had only three items with him: a copy of the United Nations Charter, the New Testament, and the Book of Psalms.

Their appeal is because they are prayers and songs. Dietrich Bonhoeffer called the psalms "the prayer book of the Bible." They are expressions of God speaking to us *and* they are also expressions of humanity responding to God. They articulate our praise and our doubts, our affirmation of God, and our frustrations with God. They give expression to the highest highs and lowest lows of our faith. The psalms speak for us; they give us the words to say when we cannot find the word to pray. Sometimes words are not enough. Our faith must be song, and the psalms put to music matters of the heart.

In this troubled and uncertain season, the Psalms will ground our faith.

OVERVIEW

A psalm is a song or hymn that was often accompanied by a stringed instrument. The Hebrew scriptures count 150 in the book of Psalms, but the ancient Greek translation of the scriptures (the Septuagint) combines a couple of them and separates a couple of them for a total of 151, which is why some modern translations will include Psalm 151.

They were written by a variety of composers and lyricists over a long period of time. There are several collections of authors. The largest collection are the songs of David, which does not mean that he wrote them but that they may have been written by officials in his royal court. Other collections were written by temple workers, such as the Korahites and Asaph. Many psalms were used in temple rituals and annual festivals, such as the Songs of Assent (Psalms 120-134) sung by Jews on pilgrimage to Jerusalem. Other collections were hymns performed for royal occasions, such as the Enthronement Psalms (93, 95-99).

You do not need to read the psalms in order. However, there are loose patterns of themes and issues that connect them into five "books:"

1. Psalms 1-41
2. Psalms 42-72
3. Psalms 73-89
4. Psalms 90-106
5. Psalms 107-150

The books are divided by doxologies (41:13; 72:19; 89:52; and 106:48), and the entire Book of Psalms ends with an entire psalm that is a doxology (150). A loose seam runs through the psalms in a book rather than a rigid order. Psalm 1 casts the general theme.

Books One, Two and Three have a loose unity. They are connected by the placement of royal psalms at the beginning of Book One (Psalm 2) and at the conclusion of Book Two (Psalm 72) and Three (Psalm 89).

Psalm Two establishes the relationship between God and the king from the line of David. Psalm 72 reaffirms this relationship. Psalm 89 begins with a detailed description of it (vv.1-37), but concludes with a description of God rejecting the covenant with David (vv.38-45) and a prayer by the rejected king (vv.45-51). There are verbal links between Psalms 42, 43 and 44 and between Psalms 73 and 74 that unite the personal alienation with the social crisis.

Books One through Three detail the failure of the covenant of David (see Psalm 89) that leads to exile. Books Two and Three instruct the community to face exile.

Books Four and Five are the response, the explanation, and the prognosis for moving forward. They answer the question of exile raised in Books One, Two and Three. God is the true home of Israel (Psalm 90) and God's enthronement (Psalms 93, 95-99).

POETRY

The poetry not always rhymes or has a fixed meter. Instead, Hebrew poetry uses parallelism in couplets and triplets. There are different kinds of parallelism in the Psalms:

- Balanced parallelism—The second line or segment of a couplet intensifies, modifies, or completes the first line or segment.
- Contrastive parallelism—The second line or segment says the opposite or draws a contrast with the first line or segment.
- Enjambment—The second line or segment completes the line of thought of the first line or segment.

HISTORY

It is helpful to know the backstory of Israel's history when reading Psalms. There are many allusions to the exodus and the wilderness experience that are touchstones for the authors and original singers of these psalms to make sense of their experiences before, during, and after the exile. Here is a timeline:

- 1000 B.C. — Reign of David; David united Israel and Judah under a single monarchy.
- 970-931 B.C. — Solomon builds the temple in Jerusalem.
- 930 B.C. — The united kingdom of Israel and Judah split into two kingdoms.
- 722 B.C. — Israel, the northern kingdom, was deported by the Assyrians.
- 701 B.C.— Assyrians conquer the city of Lachish and another deportation.

- 597 B.C. — Capture of Jerusalem and first deportation of Judah, the southern kingdom, by the Babylonians.
- 587 B.C. — Second deportation by the Babylonians; temple destroyed.
- 582 B.C. —Third deportation by the Babylonians; Babylonians appoint a governor over Judah; temple is in ruins.
- 538 B.C. —Persian King Cyrus allows the Jews to return to Jerusalem, and Nehemiah organizes the rebuilding of the city.
- 520-515 B.C. — Governor Zerubbabel rebuilds the temple.

HOW TO READ THE PSALMS

Knowing the historical and literary dimensions of the psalms is useful for having a deeper spiritual experience of reading the psalms. The aim of this study is more than learning poetry; it is to strengthen our faith. The history and the literature enhance our faith. As the old rabbinical saying goes, "To study is to pray."

It is tempting to read something in the Old Testament and immediately dismiss it because it is odd or offensive to the modern reader. Resist the temptation and look for the deeper meaning by following these steps:

1. Respect history — First ask "What was the historical context?" Then ask "How different was it from today?" And then ask "Is there a rough analogy with today?"

2. Be literary, not literal — Look for recurring words, themes, and issues. Look for patterns and be attentive to metaphors and images. Read the surrounding passages and similar passages to put it in its literary context. Remember that the Bible is made up of different kinds of material that are not always a rule or a prediction.

3. Read with God — Approach scripture with the assumption that the Spirit of God surrounds you and can speak through the Bible, even the parts we do not like.

HOW THIS STUDY WORKS

Each week, you will have a:

- **Verse for the Week:** Pick one verse from among the assigned hymns as your weekly meditation. You can choose one of the suggested verses or pick one from any of the psalms. Write it down, memorize it, read it, set it to music — whatever helps you think about. Throughout the week let God speak to you through that verse.

- **Psalm for the Day:** Each day read one psalm. Select a regular time of the day — when you wake up, during a break at work, at dinnertime, before you go to bed, or whenever. Simply read it. Maybe you will want to read it several times. There is one question for each psalm, as well as an overview of the weekly theme, to assist you.

- **Hymn for the Week:** Each week a hymn is recommended that is based on one of psalms that exemplifies the theme for the week.

Over time the daily readings of the psalms has a powerful effect on our souls. Christians over the ages have experienced this. It is my prayer that during this season in our personal and collective lives that God will deepen your faith and widen your hope.

1. **Wisdom Songs**

OVERVIEW

The book of Psalms begins with a word of wisdom in its opening psalm. Wisdom literature in the Bible was written and compiled during the heyday of the Israelite monarchy. It includes entire books, such as Job, Proverbs, and Ecclesiastes. But it also appears in several psalms and in parts of psalms. Wisdom is part of God's creative character (see Proverbs 8). Wisdom is gained through obedience to God's law and is more like learning a skill than studying a subject.

As a literary device, the psalms often contrast "the wise" with "the wicked" or "the foolish." The difference begins with how one sees reality. For the wise, they see themselves utterly dependent upon God. "Fear of the Lord" (Psalm 19:9) not only meant to show reverence but also the awareness that God alone controls our lives and the cosmos. Fools assume they are a law unto themselves.

As the Israelites saw the destruction of the temple — the central location where God was present — wisdom psalms reminded them that through obedience to the law one still had access to God, even in exile from their homeland.

A key word you will see this week and in the coming weeks is "Redeemer" (Psalm 19:14). The term derived from family relations where members bought back ("redeemed") relatives who had fallen into slavery (see Leviticus 25:47-49). Sometimes the word is translated as "next of kin" (Ruth 4:1,3). Thus, to call God your "Redeemer" denotes an intimate relationship.

VERSE OF THE WEEK

Pick one for the week and reflect on it every day this week:

- "The heavens are telling the glory of God and the firmament proclaims God's handiwork."
- "The law of the Lord is perfect, reviving the soul."
- "The fear of the Lord is pure, enduring forever."
- "Let the words of my mouth and meditation of my heart be acceptable to you, O Lord, my rock and my redeemer."
- "Take delight in the Lord and God will give you the desires of your heart."
- "Be still before the Lord and wait patiently for God."
- "Offer to God a sacrifice of thanksgiving and pay your vows to the Most High."
- "God is the strength of my heart and my portion forever."
- "Your word is a lamp to my feet and a light to my path."

DAILY READINGS AND REFLECTION QUESTIONS

Sunday — Psalm 1. How is a person who follows God's ways like a tree?

Monday — Psalm 14. How do Psalms 1 and 14 describe the difference between "the fool" and "the wise?"

Tuesday — Psalm 19. Which nurtures your awareness of God: a.) nature; b.) scripture; c.) both?

Wednesday — Psalm 37. When is it difficult to "be still before the Lord and wait patiently?"

Thursday — Psalm 49. How might having financial prosperity interfere with a person becoming wise?

Friday — Psalm 73. What does it mean to be "pure in heart?"

Saturday — Psalm 119. How do we become wise? How is this similar and different from modern education?

HYMN OF THE WEEK

"Thy Word is a Lamp" (based on Psalm 119)

2. **Personal Songs of Trust**

OVERVIEW

Some of the most beloved and famous passages in the psalms are songs of personal praise and assurance. Psalm 23 stands at the top of the list. It is both timeless and timely.

Just as you or I might use a popular hymn in our personal prayers, many of these psalms have their roots in public worship but carry personal meaning for the author. Images of God as our rock and the house of the Lord are based on the architecture of the temple being built on a rocky mount as well as the spiritual significance of God being present in the temple.

The majority of this week's selections are psalms of David which were repurposed for various occasions. Psalm 30 may have been used with Hanukkah, which celebrated the restoration of proper worship by the Maccabees in 165 B.C., and Psalm 63 may allude to the writer spending the night in the temple waiting for an answer to prayer, which came in the morning with the rising of the sun.

One of them, Psalm 131, may have been authored by a mother. This Psalm is part of the collection called the Songs of Ascent (Psalms 120-134). The Hebrew word "assent" can be a verb, "to go up," as well as a noun, the steps leading up to the city or temple. The Songs of Ascent were sung by pilgrims attending festivals in Jerusalem. They begin with a speaker outside the city (Psalm 120) and end with a benediction (Psalm 134). The mother's song was a welcome respite for the pilgrims.

Psalm 139 expresses confidence in God's ever-present love, even in "Sheol." Sheol is the underworld, the place of the dead (it is also called Abaddon in Psalm 57:11). It is not the fiery punishment of hell. Instead, Sheol is the shadowy world of non-being. Unlike other ancient near eastern literature, the Old Testament does not give details or pay much attention to Sheol, but simply notes that God can rescue us from Sheol before it is our time to die.

YOUR VERSE FOR THE WEEK

Pick one for the week and reflect on it every day:

- "The Lord is my shepherd; I shall not want."
- "The Lord is my light and my salvation; whom shall I fear?"
- "One thing I asked of the Lord, that will I seek after: to live in the house of the Lord all the days of my life and behold the beauty of the Lord."
- "Wait for the Lord; be strong and let your heart take courage; wait for the Lord."

- "Weeping may linger for the night, but joy comes with the morning."
- "You who live in the shelter of the Most High, who abide in the shadow of the Almighty, will say to the Lord, 'My refuge and my fortress'."
- "O Lord, my heart is not lifted up, my eyes are not raised too high; I do not occupy myself with things too great and too marvelous for me."
- "You hem me in, behind and before, and lay your hand upon me."
- "Where can I go from your spirit? Or where can I flee from your presence? If I ascend to heaven, you are there; if I make my bed in Sheol, you are there."
- "I praise you, for I am fearfully and wonderfully made. Wonderful are your works."

DAILY QUESTIONS

Read one psalm each day:

1. Psalm 27 — What is your greatest fear, and how might this psalm reassure you?
2. Psalm 23 — Psalm 23 is one of the most popular passages of the Bible. When have you heard it read?
3. Psalm 30 — Verse 5 says that "weeping may linger for a night, but joy comes with the morning." Is it harder for you to pray in the morning or the evening?
4. Psalm 63 — In one word, what does your "soul thirst for" right now?

5. Psalm 91 — What are the different metaphors for God in this psalm? Which one is the most meaningful for you?

6. Psalm 131 — When are you tempted to "over-think" a problem?

7. Psalm 139 — This psalm tells us that God is always with us. When have you questioned whether God was with you? How does this psalm help you reevaluate those moments in your life?

HYMN OF THE WEEK

"He Leadeth Me" (Psalm 23)

3. **Personal Prayers for Help**

OVERVIEW

Sometime the pain is so deep that we cannot say our prayers. When we cannot say them, we can sing them. The psalms set to music the deepest desires of our heart and the greatest needs in our lives.

This week's selections cover the waterfront of human troubles: Psalm 6 was for the sick, Psalm 31 was for those who mourn, and Psalm 42-43 is one song that expresses the struggle of despair. Even Jesus quoted Psalm 22.1 and 31:5 to express his predicament.

Some of the psalms reflect the struggles of David. His perilous experiences of hiding from King Saul in 1 Samuel 24 are expressed in Psalm 57. The rape of Bathsheba and the subsequent tragedies of 2 Samuel 11-12 are the backstory to his confession of sin in Psalm 51.

The temple staff were not immune to the struggles of faith.

Two selections this week, Psalm 42-43 and Psalm 88, are attributed to the Korahites. The Korahites were a temple guild of singers, gatekeepers, and bakers. Their songs were repurposed by the Jews who were forcibly deported to Babylon, which is reflected in the longing to return to the temple and the better days before the exile.

Suffering often raises the question whether it is God's wrath, as it does in Psalm 6:1. The wrath of God appears in several psalms and it is portrayed in a variety of ways and for a variety of purposes. Sometimes God's wrath is against the psalmist to discipline them (Psalms 6, 38, 88).

Other times the psalmist is requesting God to send down divine destruction on the writer's enemies to remove them (Psalms 2, 21, 56, 59, 106 and 138). Still other psalms interpret Israel's suffering as the punishment of God designed to reform the nation (Psalms 78, 79, 85 ,89 and 90). God's wrath is unleashed against the nations in Psalm 110 and 137, and God allows the full consequences of human wickedness to serve up the punishment (Psalm 76:10).

As they wrestle with the question of divine punishment, even more so do these psalms express the faithfulness of God. The imagery is rich. God is our rock, refuge, fortress; God is an eagle who shelters us under her wings.

Most of all these psalms give expression to our doubts and questions of faith. Sometimes the Bible does not speak *to* us so much as it speaks *for* us — it helps us articulate our pain and desires. The psalms give us permission to bring all those feelings and doubts into the presence of God. There is no topic that is off limits in prayer according to the examples we see in the psalms.

YOUR VERSE FOR THE WEEK

Pick one for the week and reflect on it every day):

- "As a deer longs for flowing streams, so my soul longs for you, O God."
- "Why are you cast down, O my soul, and why are you disquieted within me? Hope in God; for I shall again praise the Lord, my help and my God."
- "Turn, O Lord, save my life; deliver me for the sake of your steadfast love."
- "How long, O Lord? Will you forget me forever?"
- "Be a rock of refuge for me, a strong fortress to save me."
- "Have mercy on me, O God, according to your steadfast love; according to your abundant mercy blot out my transgressions."
- "Create in me a clean heart, O God, and put a new and right spirit within me."
- "The sacrifice acceptable to God is a broken spirit; a broken and contrite heart, O God, you will not despise."
- "My heart is steadfast, O God, my heart is steadfast. I will sing and make melody."

DAILY QUESTIONS

Read one psalm each day:

1. Psalm 42-43 — When have you felt like you were bouncing back and forth between having faith and

being overwhelmed by doubts?

2. Psalm 6 — The writer was struggling with an illness. When has an illness challenged your faith, and how did you experience God's help?

3. Psalm 13 — Have you ever asked in a moment of hardship, "How long, O God?" Did God ever answer, and if so, what was the answer and how long did it take?

4. Psalm 31 — Think of a time when you were facing a challenge. Who or what did God provide to be your "rock of refuge" and "strong fortress?"

5. Psalm 51 — What sins do you need to confess today? Use this psalm as your prayer of confession and receive God's forgiveness through the psalm.

6. Psalm 57 — What are the four metaphors for the enemy? Are any of them an apt description of opposition you have faced?

7. Psalm 88 — Have you ever felt like God was punishing you?

HYMN OF THE WEEK

"As a Deer" (Psalm 42-3)

4. Hymns of Creation and History

OVERVIEW

The psalms are more than poems about personal faith. They also express God's relationship with creation and celebrate how God works among the nations through human history. This week we explore hymns that praise the Creator and the Sovereign of history.

Hymns of creation often follow the outline of Genesis 1, such as Psalm 148. It was especially important for the Jews who were in exile to affirm that their Lord was the Creator of the universe whose just and peaceful ordering of creation was more fundamental than the domination of their captors.

Yet you can hear the influence of ancient Egyptian and Canaanite beliefs in these psalms when they mention the seas. The ancient worldview believed that creation was the result of a battle among the gods to order watery chaos. The sea and its creatures were gods to be subdued. From a Hebrew perspective they were not gods but rather objects of God's order and control. For example, the sea monster Leviathan is simply God's toy that plays in the water (Psalm 104:26).

The God who brings order out of chaos is worthy of worship. Songs such as Psalm 8 and 24 were used as liturgy performed to begin worship.

The Creator is also the liberator and judge of Israel. There is a close connection between the creation story and the saga of Israel. Hymns like Psalm 106 and 136 proclaim that God's covenant of faithful love runs through their history.

YOUR VERSE FOR THE WEEK

Pick one for the week and reflect on it every day:

- "O Lord, our Lord, how majestic is your name in all the earth."
- "The earth is the Lords and the fullness thereof."
- "God loves righteousness and justice; the earth is full of the steadfast love of the Lord."
- "Bless the Lord, O my soul."
- "O give thanks to the Lord, for God is good; God's steadfast love endures forever."

DAILY QUESTIONS

Read one psalm each day:

- Psalm 148 — How many different things or persons

are commanded to praise God?

- Psalm 8 — How are humans described?
- Psalm 24 — This hymn was sung upon entering the temple. How should we prepare for worship?
- Psalm 33 — When does nature help you feel the presence of God?
- Psalm 104 — What parts of creation do you give God thanks for?
- Psalm 106 — How was God at work in the history of the Israelites?
- Psalm 136 — How is God's work of saving the people similar to God's creative work?

HYMN OF THE WEEK

"O Worship the King" (Psalm 104) or "Let All Things Now Living" (Psalm 148 in "The Faith We Sing").

5. Royal and Prophetic Hymns

OVERVIEW

One can see that many of the psalms were crafted during the monarchial period. They are known as royal psalms because they celebrate the king. They were written and used for various royal celebrations. Psalm 21 may have been first sung to celebrate a military victory, and later used for coronations. Psalms 93 and 99 are part of a collection of enthronement songs, and Psalm 93 may have been used at the New Year's festival where God was annual enthroned. Psalm 89 commemorates the establishment of the covenant of David, which is the high mark of royal theology.

They are more than political slogans designed to defend the crown, however. They are also highly critical of unfaithful rulers, and they articulate God's standards for officials. They explain how times of national crisis, such as the exile, are God's corrective discipline for Israel. These are classified as prophetic psalms. Psalm 81 is a liturgical sermon and Psalm 94 pronounces God's judgment for wicked rulers who violate God's justice.

Justice (Hebrew, "mishpat") is the common thread connecting these songs. The Hebrew word (which is also translated "judgments" and "ordinance") appears 66 times in the psalms, and is usually linked with "righteousness" (Hebrew, "tsadaq," which is sometimes translated "justice"). God's will and power are to rightly order society with justice. Justice is both equality and compassion for the weakest members of society. When justice and righteousness are present in society, the result is peace ("shalom"), which is not only the absence of conflict but also the presence of prosperity.

The chief role of the king is to do justice (Psalm 72:4) for the weak because the Lord is the God of justice (Psalm 99:1,4). Divine approval for the monarch was conditional on their obedience to God. This was true even for David's descendants, whose dynasty was supposed to last forever based on God's covenant promises in Psalm 89.

The prophetic psalms offered the Israelites a theological explanation for exile. The loss of national independence was seen as punishment for their repeated violations of God's law that established and maintained justice. Even the enthronement psalms played a role during the exile. They reminded the people that God was still in control of their lives.

YOUR VERSE FOR THE WEEK

Pick one for the week and reflect on it every day:

- "May the ruler defend the cause of the poor of the people, give deliverance to the needy, and crush the oppressor."

- "Sing aloud to God our strength; shout for joy to the God of Jacob."
- "O that my people would listen to me."
- "I would feed you with the finest of the wheat, and with honey from the rock I would satisfy you."
- "I will sing of your steadfast love, O Lord, forever."
- "Mighty King, lover of justice, you have established equity; you have executed justice."

DAILY QUESTIONS

Read one psalm each day:

1. Psalm 72 — What is the primary responsibility of the ruler?
2. Psalm 21 — What should be the relationship between God and a public official?
3. Psalm 81 — How does this psalm describe the relationship between God and the Israelites?
4. Psalm 89 — What does God promise to David? What conditions does God place on this covenant with David's descendants?
5. Psalm 93 — The floods is a metaphor for chaos that God controls. What makes it hard for us to believe that God is in control?
6. Psalm 94 — How does this psalm describe the wicked? What is our responsibility as persons of faith?
7. Psalm 99 — How is the sovereignty of God

described? How does it compare with the responsibility of the king in Psalm 72?

HYMN OF THE WEEK

"Hail to the Lord's Anointed" (Psalm 72)

6. Communal Prayers for Help

OVERVIEW

This week we continue the focus on national and communal themes with a series of communal laments. These psalms are prayers of intercession for Israel or Jerusalem. Like last week's songs, they reflect the crisis of the exile and cast a vision of hope for their return from bondage. One can hear this in Psalms 44 and 79. Psalm 80 harkens back to the deportation of the northern kingdom, Israel, by the Assyrians. Psalm 85 may come from the experience of returning to Jerusalem after the exile and the disappointment that the glory of Jerusalem was gone. (Compare this psalm with Haggai 1 and 2.)

These psalms reaffirm God's sovereignty and faithfulness. This is expressed in Psalm 80 by calling God the "Shepherd of Israel." The shepherd was a common title for ancient kings. They hope for a new era of God's covenant love, one which harkens back to the promises made to Moses that were prior

30

to the covenant of David, which was doubted and questioned because of the exile. The psalms command the people to sing "a new song" (Psalm 85:5) to replace the Davidic theology that had failed.

These psalms emphasize our collective dependence on God and challenge us to pray and work for the well-being of our society today.

YOUR VERSE FOR THE WEEK

Pick one for the week and reflect on it every day:

- "Do not remember against us the iniquities of our ancestors; let your compassion come quickly to meet us, for we are brought very low."
- "For not in my bow do I trust, nor can my sword save me."
- "Restore us, O God of hosts; let your face shine, that we may be saved."
- "Steadfast love and faithfulness will meet; righteousness and peace will kiss each other. Faithfulness will spring up from the ground, and righteousness will look down from the sky."

DAILY QUESTIONS

Read one psalm each day:

1. Psalm 79 — Why is Jerusalem destroyed?
2. Psalm 44 — What are nations not to put their trust in?

3. Psalm 60 — How is God described in this psalm?

4. Psalm 80 — How should we pray for our nation?

5. Psalm 83 — The writer prays for Israel's enemies to be defeated. How should we pray for other nations?

6. Psalm 85 — What is your vision of hope for our city? Our state? Our nation? Our world?

7. Psalm 144 — What do you think is God's relationship to human warfare?

HYMN OF THE WEEK

"This is My Song"

7. Communal Songs of Praise

OVERVIEW

We end our study of the psalms on a high note. This week we celebrate God's love and glory with communal songs of praise. Many of these are found in Books Four and Five because these last two books are an answer to the crisis of the exile which dominates Books Two and Three. They offer hope after the crisis. The call to sing "new songs" is repeated in Psalm 98. We are commanded to praise God in Psalms 117. Psalm 148 is one of the hallelujah psalms because the Hebrew "hallelujah" (translated "Praise the Lord") is used 11 times.

Some of them have been the source of our best-known hymns. For example, Psalm 46 is the basis for "A Mighty Fortress is Our God." The hymn tune "Old 100th" gets its name from Psalm 100, which is set to music in "All People That on Earth Do Dwell."

YOUR VERSE FOR THE WEEK

Pick one for the week and reflect on it every day):

- "O sing to the Lord a new song, for God has done marvelous things."
- "God is our refuge and strength, a very present help in trouble."
- "God is in the midst of the city; it shall not be moved. God will help it when the mourning dawns."
- "Make a joyful noise to God, all the earth."
- For the Lord is good; God's love endures forever, and God's faithfulness to all generations."
- "Praise the Lord!"

DAILY QUESTIONS

Read one psalm each day:

1. Psalm 98 — What does the writer praise God for?
2. Psalm 46 — What should we give God thanks for in our church?
3. Psalm 66 — This psalm recounts God's deliverance from Egypt. For what should we give God thanks about our collective history?
4. Psalm 100 — How does giving thanks to God comfort and reassure us?
5. Psalm 117 — Put this psalm into your own words.
6. Psalm 147 — What is your favorite hymn of praise?
7. Psalm 150 — Which musical instruments help you feel close to God?

HYMNS OF THE WEEK

"A Mighty Fortress Is Our God" (Psalm 46)

"We Sing to You, O God" (Psalm 66, in "The Faith We Sing")

"Joy to the World" (Psalm 98)

"All People That on Earth Do Dwell" (Psalm 100)

"From All That Dwell Below the Skies" (Psalm 117)

"Praise the Lord Who Reigns Above" (Psalm 150)

"Praise to the Lord, the Almighty" (Psalm 150)

About the Author

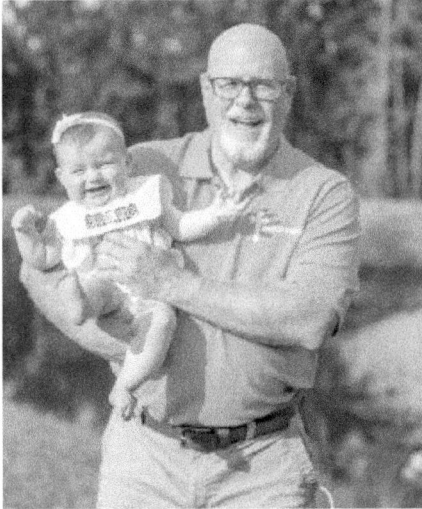

Darren Cushman Wood is the senior pastor of North United Methodist Church in Indianapolis, Indiana. He has served small and large, rural and urban United Methodist churches for over 30 years. He is a graduate of the University of Evansville and Union Theological Seminary.

He is the author of two books, hymns, and numerous articles. He is an adjunct professor of labor studies at Indiana University. He is married to Ginny and as of this writing they have three adult children and one grandchild.

The North Study Series